Little Pebble™

Our Families

Grandmothers
Are Part of a Family

by Lucia Raatma

CAPSTONE PRESS
a capstone imprint

Little Pebble is published by Capstone Press,
1710 Roe Crest Drive, North Mankato, Minnesota 56003
www.mycapstone.com

**Library of Congress Cataloging-in-Publication Data is available
on the Library of Congress website**

ISBN: 978-1-5157-7454-9 (library binding)
ISBN: 978-1-5157-7467-9 (paperback)
written by Lucia Raatma

Editorial Credits
Christianne Jones, editor; Juliette Peters, designer;
Wanda Winch, media researcher; Laura Manthe, production specialist

Photo Credits
Capstone Studio: Karon Dubke, 7, 9, 17; Shutterstock: Angelina Babii, paper texture,
Blend Images, 21, CroMary, 15, digitalskillet, 13, Kamira, cover, Monkey Business Images,
5, NadyaEugene, 11, nafterphoto, 1, SpeedKingz, 19, Teguh Mujiono, tree design

Table of Contents

Grandmothers

A grandmother is the mother
of your father or mother.
She can be called grandma.

A grandma may have grandsons. She may also have granddaughters.

What Grandmothers Do

Mia's grandma is a doctor.

She helps sick people.

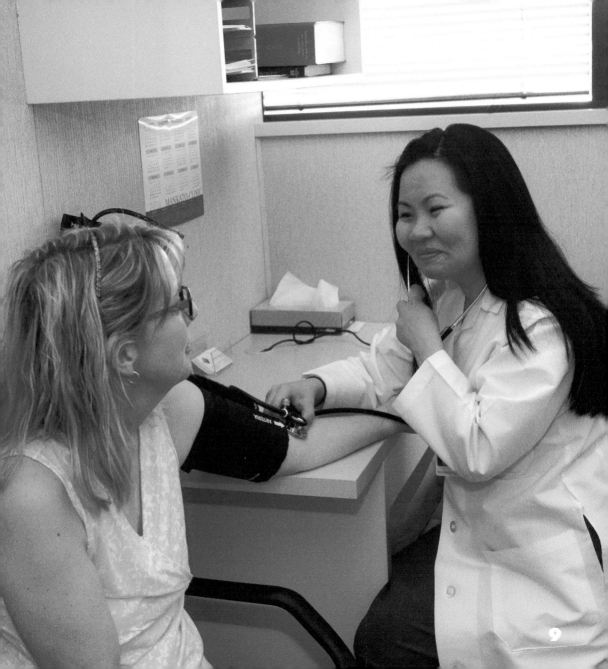

Noah's grandma lives
by the beach. They look
for shells.

Carter's grandma uses
the computer. He helps.

Emma lives with her grandma. They like to bake.

Beth's grandma likes
to make things.
She teaches Beth.

Robert's mom is at work.

Robert's grandma takes

him to school.

Grandmas hug.

They kiss.

They love.

Glossary

bake—to cook in an oven

doctor—a person trained to treat sick or injured people

granddaughter—a female child of one's son or daughter

grandmother—the mother of a mother or father

grandson—a male child of one's son or daughter

Read More

Ajmera, Maya. *Our Grandparents: A Global Album.* Watertown, MA: Charlesbridge, 2010.

Harris, Robie H. *Who's in My Family?* All About Our Families. Somerville, MA: Candlewick, 2012.

Hunter, Nick. *Finding Out About Your Family History.* Mankato, MN: Heinemann-Raintree, 2015.

Internet Sites

FactHound offers a safe, fun way to find Internet sites related to this book. All of the sites on FactHound have been researched by our staff.

Here's all you do:
Visit *www.facthound.com*
Type in this code: 9781515774549

 Check out projects, games and lots more at
www.capstonekids.com

Index